PHARMACISTS

PEOPLE WHO CARE FOR OUR HEALTH

Robert James

The Rourke Book Co., Inc.
Vero Beach, Florida 32964

C.1 1998

Library of Congress Cataloging-in-Publication Data

James, Robert, 1942-
    Pharmacists / by Robert James.
      p. cm. — (People who care for our health)
    Includes index.
    Summary: Describes what pharmacists do, where they work,
and how they train and prepare for their jobs.
    ISBN 1-55916-171-X
    1. Pharmacy—Vocational guidance—Juvenile literature.
[1. Pharmacy—Vocational guidance. 2. Occupations.
3. Vocational guidance]
I. Title II. Series: James, Robert, 1942- People who care for our
health
RS92.J35   1995
615'.1'023—dc20
                                  95–18939
                                      CIP
                                      AC

Printed in the USA

TABLE OF CONTENTS

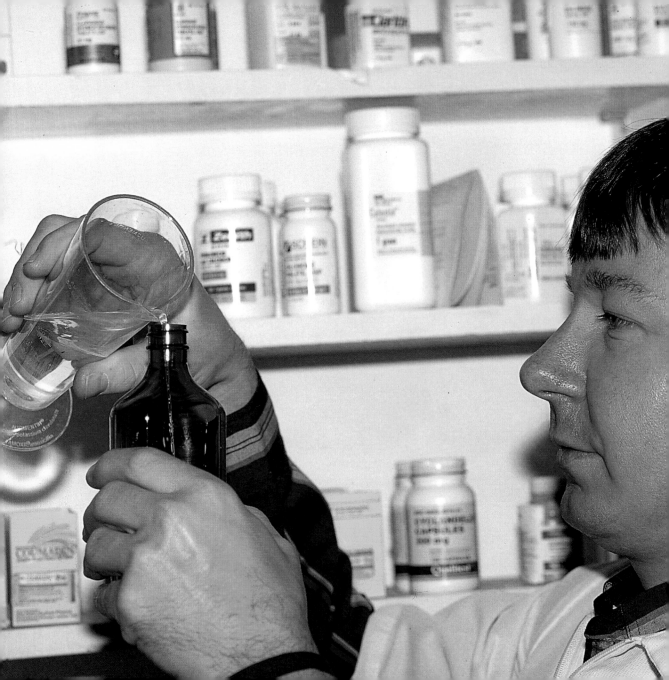

PHARMACISTS

Injured and ill people often need drugs, or medicines, to regain their health. Often, a doctor or dentist decides the kind and amount of medicine a person should take.

A pharmacist, or druggist, prepares medicine from a doctor's or dentist's request, called a **prescription** (pre SCRIP shun). Pharmacists are experts in knowing how drugs work. A pharmacist helps explain to people what to expect from their medicine.

Pharmacists, or druggists, are experts in the preparing of medicines

WHAT PHARMACISTS DO

In addition to preparing drugs, pharmacists keep detailed records of drug sales, label drugs, and offer advice.

Drugs for sale in the aisles of drugstores do not require a doctor's prescription. These drugs are called "over-the-counter" drugs because they can be bought easily, like a pack of gum, without a doctor's okay. But they are still drugs, and they must be used properly.

The pharmacist can help people choose the most useful over-the-counter drugs.

Among other things, computers tell pharmacists who is using what medicine and for how long

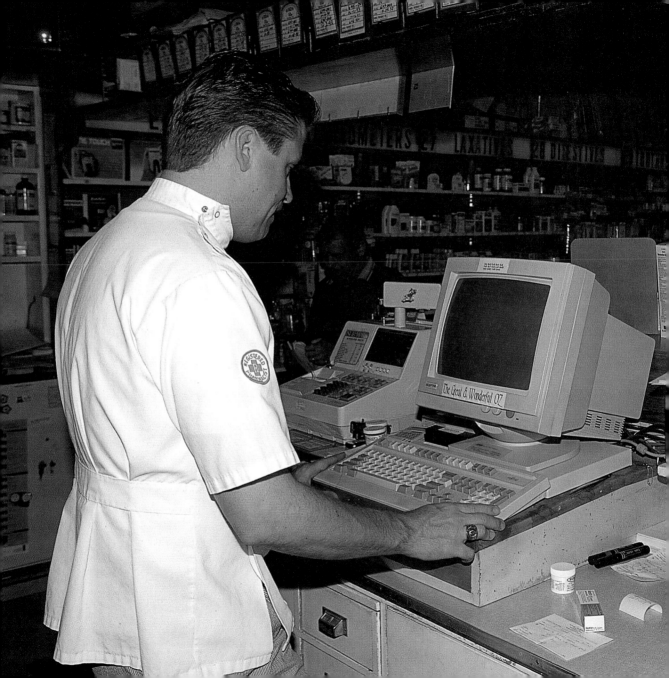

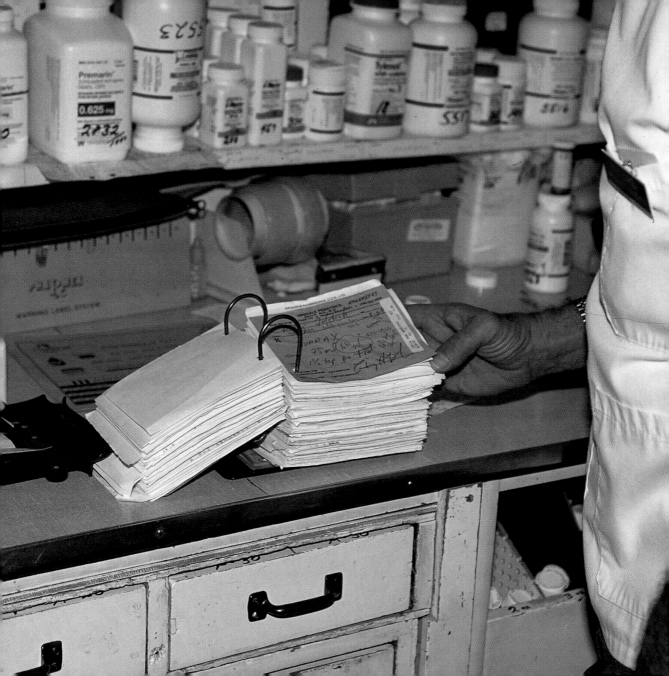

PRESCRIPTIONS

Doctors and dentists write prescriptions to order drugs for patients who need them. Prescriptions involve powerful drugs that need to be taken with great care. Pharmacists keep prescription drugs behind their counter to control their sale and use.

The prescription itself tells a pharmacist which drug to prepare and in what amount. It also tells the patient how to take the drug and how often to take it.

The pharmacist prepares the drug and a label for the drug container.

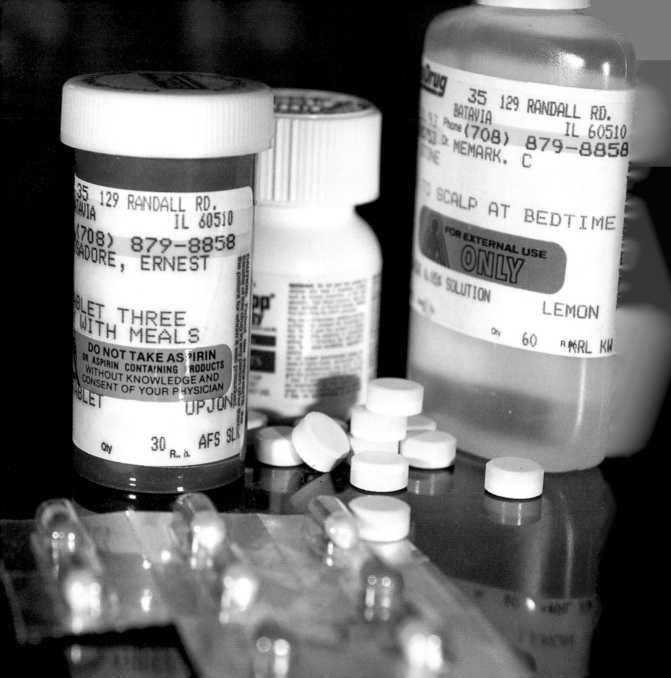

DRUG LABELS

The small label on a drug container is full of important information. It names the drug. It tells how much the patient should take and when. The label may tell how to take the drug, perhaps with a meal.

The label tells whether the patient can refill the prescription and what **side effects** (SIDE eh FEHX) a patient might expect. Side effects are unwanted changes in the way someone's mind or body works.

Drug labels should always be left on their containers to avoid mix-ups.

Drug labels list important information, and they should always be left attached to the drug containers

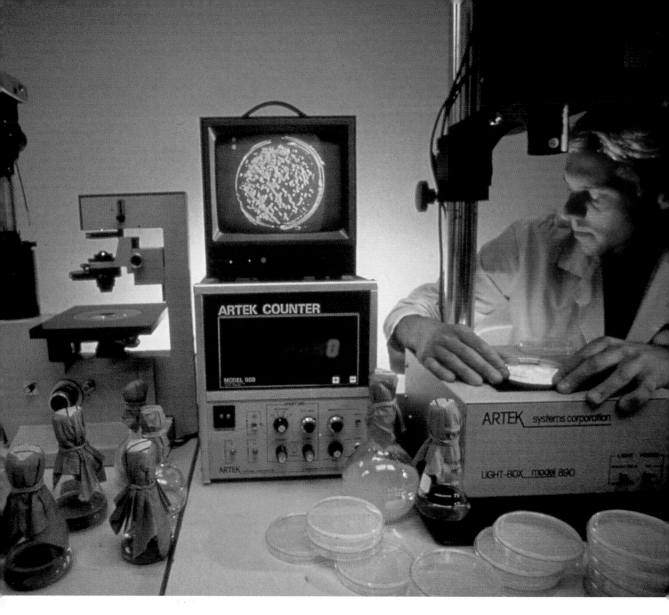

Laboratory research ensures that pharmacists will have more and better drugs to sell in the future

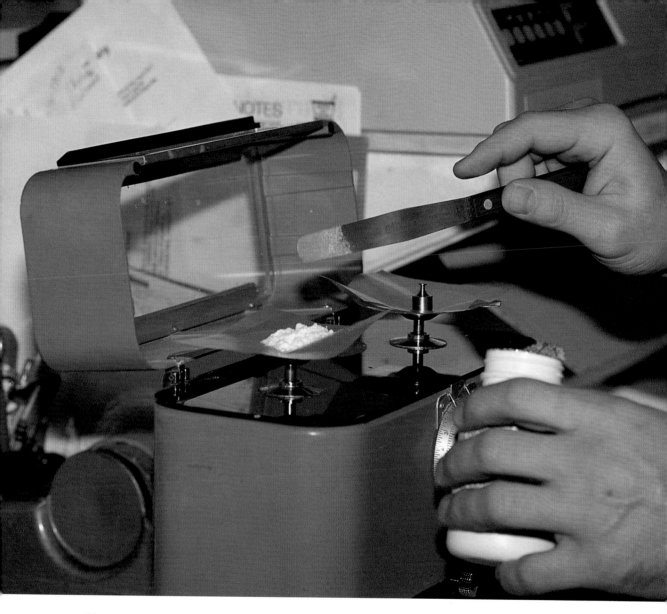

Pharmacists sometimes have to weigh medicines, such as this powder drug, before packaging them

PRESCRIPTION DRUGS

Drugs ordered by doctors and dentists for their patients are **legal** (LEE gull) drugs. They are substances that are used either to treat or prevent illness. Legal drugs save thousands of lives. They also help sick and injured people be more comfortable than they would be without drugs.

However, any drug can be dangerous. Even a common, useful drug, such as aspirin, can kill if it is used improperly.

Scientists at drug companies work in carefully controlled conditions to produce medicines

PREPARING PRESCRIPTIONS

Drugs come in many forms. A drug can be powder, liquid, cream, ointment, tablet, mist, capsule, or patch. A patch is applied to someone's skin, like a bandage. The medicine works its way from the patch through the skin and into the body.

A pharmacist prepares a prescription by measuring out the correct amount of drug and placing it in a container.

Pharmacists count or measure prescription drugs and package them

WHERE PHARMACISTS WORK

Pharmacists work in **pharmacies** (FARM uh sees), or drugstores. A pharmacy may be a separate store, or it may be part of a larger building. Several big North American supermarkets and department stores have drugstores under their roofs. Hospitals and medical **clinics** (KLIN ihks) usually have drugstores, too.

Pharmacies usually stock magazines, greeting cards, cosmetics, and small gift items along with a variety of health care products.

Pharmacy shelves are stocked with prescription drugs behind the pharmacist's counter

THE PHARMACIST'S HELPERS

Pharmacists work closely with doctors and dentists, naturally. Pharmacists also work closely with salespeople who work for drug companies.

Pharmacists don't **manufacture** (man u FAX ur), or make, drugs. Drug companies make drugs. Pharmacists buy drugs from these companies. The company salespeople tell pharmacists and doctors about new drugs that are available.

Many pharmacists hire helpers called pharmacy technicians. The job of filling the prescriptions, however, remains in the druggist's hands.

Drug companies manufacture and pack drugs for pharmacies to sell

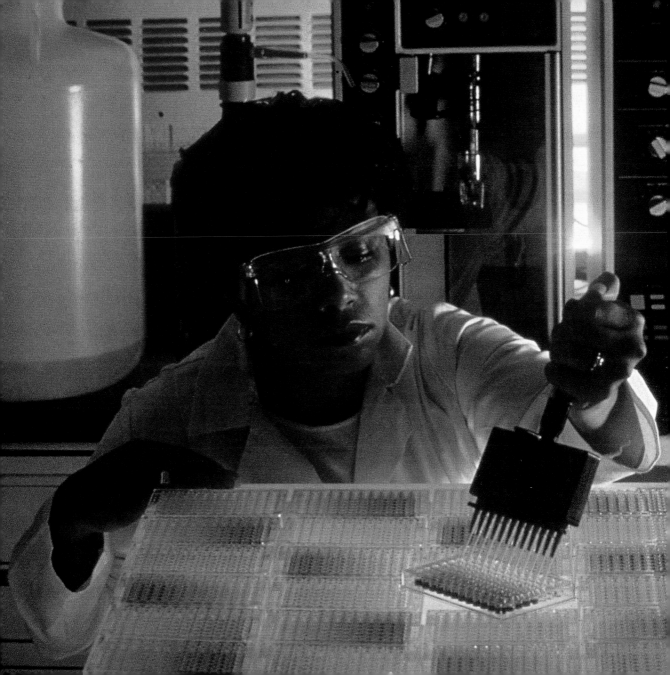

BECOMING A PHARMACIST

Pharmacists have at least five years of college studies. They earn a degree in **pharmacy** (FARM uh see). Pharmacy is the practice of preparing and knowing how to use prescription drugs.

Many pharmacists enroll in a six- or seven-year college program. That program permits them to work closely with hospital doctors and design complicated drug treatments.

Each pharmacist passes a state test before actually working as a pharmacist.

Glossary

clinic (KLIN ihk) — a place, usually with several doctors, for treating large numbers of patients who don't need overnight care

legal (LEE gull) — anything that is done within the law; not against the law

manufacture (man u FAX ur) — to make, especially in large numbers by machine

pharmacies (FARM uh sees) — drugstores

pharmacy (FARM uh see) — the study and science of preparing legal drugs; a drugstore

prescription (pre SCRIP shun) — a doctor's or dentist's order for drugs to be taken by a patient

side effects (SIDE eh FEHX) — unwanted physical or mental results caused by a drug

INDEX